STRENGTH RENOVATION

Rebuilding Faith Communities

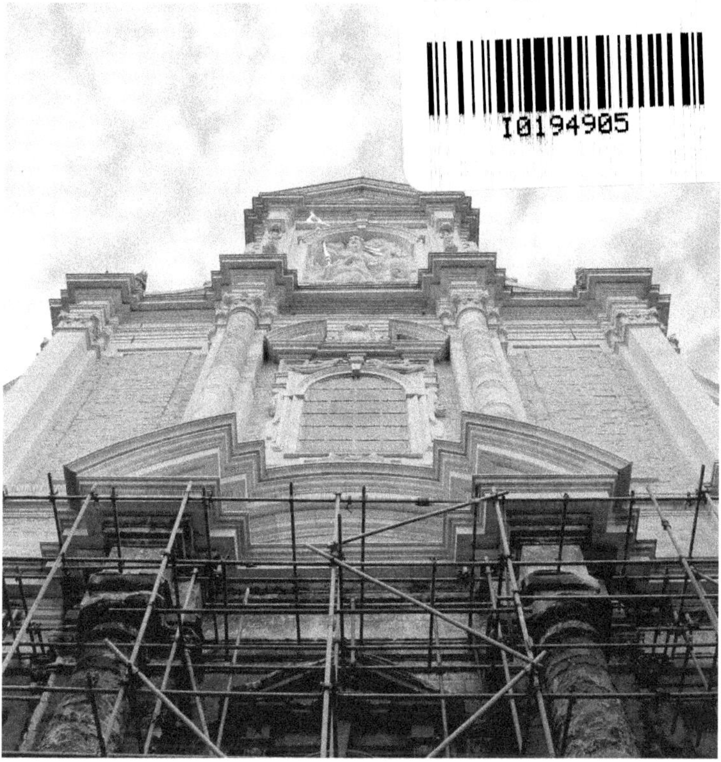

DR. NICK PALMIERI

LIBERTY UNIVERSITY Press

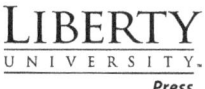

Strength Renovation
Rebuilding Faith Communities
by Dr. Nick Palmieri

© Copyright 2011 Nicholas V. Palmieri. All rights reserved. No portion of this book may be reproduced by any means, electronic or mechanical, including photocopying, recording, or by any information storage retrieval system, without permission of the copyright's owner, except for the inclusion of brief quotations for a review.

Back cover photo by:
Kristi Mangan Photography
www.kmanganphoto.com

ISBN 13: 978-1-935986-09-6

nvp@nickpalmieri.com

Press
Lynchburg, Va.

www.liberty.edu/libertyuniversitypress

Scripture quotations noted NIV are from the HOLY BIBLE: NEW INTERNATIONAL VERSION®. Copyright © 1973, 1978, 1984 by International Bible Society. Used by permission of Zondervan Publishing House. All rights reserved

Dedicated to

Emma Lynnell and Caleb Daniel Palmieri
My two heaven-sent grandchildren

Contents

Preface

Part One: Strength Renovation
1. A Community Parable 15
2. Renovation Signs 19
3. Pardon our Mess 25
4. The Master Architect 31

Part Two: Supercharged Personal Stewardship
5. Discovery 39
6. Five Loaves and Two Fish 47
7. The Ultimate Makeover 55

Part Three: Supercharged Community Stewardship
8. Community Discovery 61
9. Community Coordination 71
10. Preventive Maintenance 75
11. Optimal Growth 79

Renovation Reflections

Resources

The Lord's renovation plan directs us to make a shift from focusing on each other's weaknesses to seeing His reflection in each other's *strengths*.

Preface

In the spring of 2009, I learned about renovation at the Cleveland Clinic in Ohio. My mitral heart valve had a serious problem — some of the chordae (heart strings) holding the valve in place ruptured. My blood was backing up, my heart valve needed to be strengthened, and time was running out.

A dear friend encouraged me to find the best care possible, even if it meant traveling across the country. I invested hours online looking for the preeminent physician and facility for my condition, until I found a surgeon who specializes in heart valve repairs. Dr. Mark Gillinov performed the repair using the da Vinci Surgical System[1] and replaced the ruptured heart strings with artificial ones. The same company that manufactures dental floss and guitar strings makes artificial heart strings, so in theory, my life now hangs by a few threads! My heart renovation is similar to an architectural one. The "building" did not require removal and replacement. It needed restoration to its original design.

It is amazing to see how architectural renovations restore old buildings to their former glory. Built in 1925, the Vinoy was the premier hotel in St. Petersburg, Florida. The hotel's timeless, elegant design graced the downtown area like a jewel by the sun-soaked, picturesque bay. However, the gem of St. Pete slowly deteriorated over the years and closed its doors in 1974.[2] The building stood vacant until the 1990's when it was lovingly restored to its original magnificence. Each time I walk into the lobby of this majestic structure, I get a sense of something wonderful in the midst of our "throw away" culture. Instead of discarding the old hotel like a disposable razor, two corporations restored the Vinoy to its original grandeur through a 93 million dollar financial commitment. Renovation does not come cheap; nevertheless, it is worth every penny!

God wants His community of believers to keep their original magnificence and flourish through consistent, life-giving renewal. However, many churches are not flourishing. In fact, much like a neglected building deteriorates over time, they are falling apart. How then does one recognize the need for strength renovation? A careful look at a faith community's structure provides a few hints. Problems ranging from conflict within a group of believers, increasing numbers of people leaving, and church divisions or splits give us an indication of decline. The integrity of the community suffers through a deteriorating support system, just like the failing structural support of the Vinoy Hotel. A strong support system helps faith communities maintain their structural integrity through sound, encouraging relationships. The quality of our relationships is the central focus for strength renovation. More specifically, the Lord's renovation plan requires us to make a shift from focusing on each other's weaknesses to seeing his reflection in each other's strengths. It is essential to fully appreciate our potential, just like the investors who looked at a broken, abandoned hotel envisioned the Vinoy in its former glory. One way to bring about this type of renovation is to consider the fact that God has given each of us specific strengths, gifts, and talents. The ability to visualize a building's potential comes from focusing on the beauty beneath its imperfect appearance. Renovation begins with a discovery of what He's given and a consideration of its hidden splendor; it continues when we acknowledge and value this treasure in others.

If your faith community is experiencing conflict and possible division, strength renovation offers hope for restoration and renewal. If, on the other hand, your faith community is currently thriving, consider using the principles of strength renovation as a strategy for continuous spiritual development — maintaining a strong, healthy faith community requires diligent care. Strength renovation will help you focus on what you need for consistent, meaningful growth.

God wants His community of believers to keep their original magnificence and flourish through consistent, life-giving *renewal.*

"... I will return and rebuild David's fallen tent. Its ruins I will rebuild and I will restore it, that the remnant of men may seek the Lord, and all the Gentiles who bear my name, says the Lord who does these things." Acts 15:16-17

PART ONE
Strength Renovation

Chapter One
A Community Parable

The Story

There once was a small group of believers who came together to start a church. Excitement and joy supplied energy and a strong sense of purpose. In the beginning, they enjoyed each other's company and worked together in pursuit of a dream. Families frequently met for picnics and other activities. Special projects spontaneously captured the group's interest; they made significant contributions to their community.

After being together for a few years, the sense of purpose began to fade and internal conflicts strained relationships. Without realizing what was happening, those in dispute gathered people to support their cause and the turf wars began. A perceptual shift changed how they related to each other and faultfinding became a routine activity. Those who once provided support now focused on individual imperfections. Self-righteousness compromised their love. The group split, friendships were broken and many left in a confused state, wondering how all this ill will ever began. Some acquired a deficit-focused perception that infiltrated their relationships with other people, including their relationship with a loving Father who calls us to accept and support each other. The community that once provided support and meaning became a painful memory.

The community that once provided support and meaning became a painful memory.

What Happened?

Let's consider what happened in our scenario to gain a better understanding of the downward spiral of dissension. The initial excitement of a new adventure began with group members trusting God for direction; they clearly recognized their dependence on the Lord. After achieving some success, the "Galatians Syndrome" began to take hold. The Galatians Syndrome reflects what happened to the church at Galatia, when they began by faith but did not continue to walk by faith. In time, they came to believe their own reasoning and good intentions would complete the work. What first began as joyful trust morphed into frustrating self-reliance. In our parable, the frustration evidenced itself through blaming others and escalated to a self-righteous attitude. Strong personalities clashed, people began to take up sides, and the turf wars were in full force. At this point, it was only a matter of time until the group split, and pointing the finger of judgment and malicious conversation became a regular practice that clearly violated the principal of Isaiah 58:9-10.

"Then you will call, and the LORD will answer; you will cry for help, and he will say: Here am I. If you do away with the yoke of oppression, with the *pointing finger* and *malicious talk,* and if you spend yourselves in behalf of the hungry and satisfy the needs of the oppressed, then your light will rise in the darkness, and your night will become like the noonday." Isaiah 58:9-10

Chapter Two
Renovation Signs

What are the signs demonstrating a need for strength renovation? The following indicators provide a picture of community deterioration.

GRATITUDE DEFICIT:
- Not recognizing or being thankful for the numerous blessings in our lives
- Expecting God and others to serve us and meet our needs
- Focusing on what is wrong with people and life circumstances

LOVE DEFICIT:
- Difficulty focusing on the needs of others – inability to give and receive love

JOY DEFICIT:
- Happiness eludes us and is difficult to find

PATIENCE DEFICIT:
- Low tolerance for waiting and quick to judge

PEACE DEFICIT:
- Frequent stress and difficulty resting in God
- Expecting the worst and excessive worry

SELF RELIANCE:
- Becoming disillusioned through our disappointments and trusting in ourselves without asking for help from God or others

SELF RIGHTEOUSNESS:
- Embracing a false belief of earning our righteousness and therefore being qualified to judge

The "renovation signs" listed above are indicators of a deficit-focused perspective, where we fail to see the strengths of others and acquire tunnel vision. Scrutinizing each other from a deficit perspective is an ungodly activity that sets the stage for a series of predictable events. First, we become blind to the goodness of people, ignore their strong points and amplify their weaknesses. This attitude is accompanied by negative expectations and relating to others in a condescending, judgmental manner. Second, a defensive response from those we judge counters our emotional attack. In turn, they look for our weaknesses, causing a downward spiral of negativity that destroys fellowship and makes our love for others grow cold. Third and finally, our negativity may turn inward and cause us to lose the joy once found in our relationship with God. Furthermore, we may even believe that God's focus is on our weaknesses, leading to self-condemnation and a sense of alienation from our loving Father. Condemnation offers no remedy and leads to despair, which in turn leaves us without hope and alienated from God and our sisters and brothers.

Recognizing Our Need for Repair

Albert Einstein said "a problem well defined is half solved." Once deterioration in a faith community is detected, two options are available. Disgruntled and hurt, you may choose apathy and simply ignore what's happening, or decide to take action toward repair. Review the renovation signs and consider how you can move closer to God. Your focus throughout this process should be on developing an attitude of gratitude, asking the Lord to help you move from morbid self-preoccupation to selfless love.

Renovation begins once you understand the need to make a shift from focusing on weaknesses to seeing God's reflection in each other's strengths.

"A problem well-stated is a problem half-solved." –*Albert Einstein*

Chapter Three
Pardon our Mess

Preparation

How then can a community of believers set the stage for making a shift from a deficit perspective to one that is strength-based? To answer this question, let's take a closer look at a deficit-focused environment. Our consumer driven society is in direct opposition to heaven's selfless, giving nature. Any society driven by consumption promotes individual happiness above all else and fosters a sense of discontentment. Individuals usurp God's place as the center of the universe and are consequently driven by the influence of what I call the "me first pest," otherwise known as "Ego Maximus." Once our faith communities are infested with this ungodly bug, healthy relationships are systematically destroyed. We want what we want, when we want it, and our instant gratification environment feeds the ego-driven pest.

Infestation indicators include being quick to complain about minor inconveniences and losing touch with the virtue of patience. It evidences itself through the thoughts and actions of unthankful children, addicted to fulfilling perceived needs. The message is clear: you will not be complete until you purchase a particular product, the new improved product, the new version of the new improved product, and so forth. The combination of selfish tendencies, along with support from a consumer-based society leads us to focus on what is missing in our lives. This ungodly mix of discontentment translates to a deficit view of our world. Our focus is on what is missing, instead of all the blessings He provides.

Pest Control

Thank God for His "pest control services" and unconditional guarantee. Jesus provided the remedy for Ego Maximus using the two greatest commandments: love God and love your neighbor as yourself. The first act of making the transition from a deficit to a strength-based perspective is to shift our focus. Looking to God to validate our worth and satisfy our need for meaning creates a value system opposed to popular culture.[3] That is, our significance is determined by virtue of His love for us; it is not derived from wealth or position.

The new self is a reflection of His goodness (Ephesians 4:24).

Awakening to the concept of love based on who God is and how He perceives us, we enter into a transformational experience to accept ourselves and see God's reflection in all creation.

This shift may be most difficult for the individual indoctrinated to focus solely on the sinful nature. When someone tells me I must die to myself because self is deplorable and destitute, my response is this: "are you referring to my old self or the new self?" There is an old self that is opposed to God. However, even in the old self, or the fallen state of man, one may see a faint image of God's goodness. The person who receives Christ as Savior becomes a new creation, old things have passed away and all things become new (2 Corinthians

5:17). The new self is a reflection of His goodness (Ephesians 4:24). Seeing ourselves from God's perspective frees us to see others more clearly. Our heavenly Father knows our potential; He is completely cognizant of what we can be. The hope of being transformed into His ideal design opens our eyes to discern the same potential in others. Once the building called faith community is free of ego-driven pests, Jesus, the Master Architect, begins the renovation process.

Jesus provided the remedy for Ego Maximus using the two greatest commandments: *love God and love your neighbor as yourself.*

Chapter Four
The Master Architect

The Lord is the one who orchestrates faith community renovation. Keeping a clear line of communication with Him cultivates a deep appreciation for quality design, construction, and project completion. He knows exactly what needs to be done, who needs to do it, and the timing for each phase of the project. He empowers us to complete the work.

Hebrews chapter 11 provides hints about how God sees us. Abraham, the great man of faith, is described in this passage. His faith and influence on history are honored; however, something is missing from the account. Abraham lied on occasion in an attempt to save his own life, with no regard to how his sin would affect others. Why would the Lord not remind us of Abraham's shortcomings in Hebrews? King David also made some major mistakes, yet he is called a man after God's heart. Moreover, Peter denied Christ, yet he was one of the three men closest to the Lord, even though Jesus knew his character flaws.

How then does God look at those who place their trust in him? He separates our sins from us as far as the east is from the west, and buries them in the depth of the seas. He calls us the righteousness of God in Christ and a new creation. The Lord is resolute in renovating our lives, and chooses not to recall our shortcomings. He focuses on our potential.

What are the benefits of a strength-based approach? First, an awareness of what is good about people helps us communicate in an accepting, nonjudgmental manner. Strengths are maximized, weaknesses minimized, and a positive model of mutual respect initiates relational change. The upward spiral of positivity builds fellowship and strengthens our love for each other. Moreover, positivity turned inward generates great joy in seeing the goodness of God in our lives.

Recognizing our God-given strengths gives birth to a hope that encourages us to flourish, as we are free to become His envisioned vessel of honor.[4]

God is the Master Architect of strength renovation. By virtue of His creative power, each and every person possesses an array of distinct gifts and talents (Psalm 139 and 1 Corinthians 12). We are individuals created to honor the Lord with our talents. More specifically, you and I are part of an answer to a prayer Jesus spoke to His father when He said, "Thy kingdom come. Thy will be done on earth, as it is in heaven." Bringing a touch of heaven to earth is our God-given mission. This plan is supported by a simple, miraculous concept. Becoming the person God wants us to be equips us to make a one-of-a-kind contribution to the world. God intends to leverage the talents and gifts of His people to bless others by demonstrating His unparalleled character through the good works of His chosen.

Discovering our God-given talents is a lifelong adventure, and requires an open mind and heart. This journey of discovery takes courage to acknowledge our gifts and come face to face with the calling of meaningful service. Uncovering our own talents is only one part of the divine adventure; we also enjoy the privilege of encouraging others in the discovery and fruitful exercise of their own unique gifts.

God's plan for us is both individualistic and corporate. He is a God of hope who sees the potential in His children; however, His sons and daughters live in a broken world filled with pessimism and unbelief. They live in a deficit-focused society, ever scanning the environment for possible land mines. Upon considering God's solution-focused approach to life, His children begin to realize the Savior's intention to renovate their existence through strength and courage.

Strength renovation calls for replacing injurious behaviors with new ones infused with godliness.

Strength renovation calls for replacing injurious behaviors with new ones infused with godliness. It calls upon recognition of God's character in our lives and seeing His individualized handiwork in our gifts and talents. It is acknowledging God's best within us, and within our newly created life in Christ Jesus. It is good overcoming evil — God's power in our lives kicks our old nature to the curb. Faith overwhelms doubt, love overpowers hate, peace eclipses anxiety, and hope replaces discouragement. Spiritual growth evidences itself through new vision and insight of how Christ's goodness is reflected in our lives.

We are part of an answer to a prayer Jesus spoke to His father when He said *"Thy kingdom come. Thy will be done on earth, as it is in heaven."*

*Bringing a touch of heaven to earth is
our God-given mission.*

PART TWO
Supercharged Personal Stewardship

Chapter Five
Discovery

"Supercharged stewardship" reveals God's reflection in our individual lives. It is the discovery and use of our God-given talents and has two essential components. The first component is a strength-focused personal assessment to discover our God-given gifts, and the second includes using those gifts to bring a touch of heaven to earth. We are designed for meaningful service. His Spirit gives us power and supercharges our ability to make an eternal difference.

There is something quite wonderful about discovering one's talents. A few years ago, my wife Terry and I developed an interest in stained glass and discussed the possibility of taking classes to learn how to make glass creations. We were extremely fortunate to learn of a gentleman who provided lessons in his home studio; he taught no more than four students at a time. During those lessons, our experience was more of an apprenticeship than a stained glass class. I will never forget our first evening session with the master artisan. Terry and I began with a piece of clear glass. Our instructor demonstrated how to score the glass and then break it with gentle pressure. We approached the task with hesitation; my hands were shaking. I scored the glass and could not believe how easily it divided into two pieces. During the next few weeks, the artist walked us through a series of skill sets needed to produce a finished product. He stretched us beyond what we thought was possible. We proudly displayed our first projects in our home. Both Terry and I were amazed at how much we learned from our instructor and friend, and how we discovered our talent for stained glass art. About a year later, we entered a stained glass piece in a national contest. Our stained glass fruit bowl claimed national recognition as a superb piece of glasswork. The feelings which accompanied winning the contest included exhilaration, surprise, and the joy associated with our newly discovered talent. My wife and I wanted to share this joy with others and began making stained glass gifts for our friends.

Talent discovery brings new life and great joy. I felt so alive when working with glass and completing a project. The act of creating is something we inherit from our heavenly Father. Discovering our God-given talents not only brings us to life, it also prompts us to share the wealth. Enjoying the sense of operating in our high level skills engenders generosity, and God richly blesses those who freely give their best.

The first step in using our gifts wisely (i.e., personal stewardship) is the discovery of those gifts. To help you with this process, you can take an assessment, ask your friends, or simply reflect on positive comments

Talent discovery brings new life and great joy.

from others and focus on where your greatest joy meets the world's greatest need. Two excellent assessments for spiritual gifts include Network from Willowcreek and SHAPE from Saddleback Church.[5,6] Two valuable resources for strength discovery are Strengths Finder (http://www.strengthsfinder.com) and Values in Action (http://www.viacharacter.org).[7,8]

Your strengths may remain undetected for several reasons. For one, if you define strengths and gifts as something spectacular, or even miraculous, you will miss what God treasures. The Fruit of the Spirit (Galatians 5:22) for example, includes love, joy, peace, patience, kindness, goodness, faithfulness, gentleness and self-control. These are some of the strengths God is actively forming in our lives. If you see the fruit of the Spirit as "all or nothing," you will fail to recognize incremental change. However, viewing the fruit of the Spirit as characteristics God progressively develops in our lives gives us an appreciation of how patiently He changes us to become more like His Son.

The Values in Action Survey provides wonderful insight for strength discovery. Character strengths include creativity, love of learning, bravery, perseverance, honesty, zest, the capacity to love and be loved, kindness, teamwork, fairness, forgiveness and mercy, humility, self-regulation, gratitude, hope, and humor.

The Law of Expedition

Discovery is oftentimes serendipitous. Exploring uncharted territory may unearth something quite different from our initial intention. My own life-threatening heart condition was discovered during a visit to the doctor after contracting pneumonia. Penicillin, cellophane, and sticky notes were all unexpected discoveries, with imperfection as one of the key ingredients to each breakthrough. Columbus is a prime example of a fabulous foible; unlike most men, he became famous for his lack of direction. The discovery of penicillin required an untidy lab. A failed attempt to create a plastic-covered tablecloth birthed cellophane, and sticky notes resulted from an unsuccessful attempt at creating a strong adhesive.

Discovering our strengths is an excursion into unexplored territory. Before beginning the adventure, it may be necessary to overcome possible hindrances to taking the first steps. Fear of leaving old familiar habits, experiencing anxiety over not being equipped to deal with new discoveries, or perhaps a fear of accountability prevent us from leaving our place of safety. On the other hand, the excursion may be viewed as an adventure leading to more opportunities for a better quality of life. Longing for the possibility of discovering new strengths for more effective service, or realizing the season of our discontentment is a friend who leads us to venture into God's best, embolden us to step out of the boat and walk toward the One who calls us to miraculous faith.

Identifying our strengths can prove to be challenging, especially if our life is defined in terms of what is missing. However, since the Father is the giver of every good and perfect gift His work is displayed in that which He gives. He gives us gifts and a righteous character to reflect His light to those who wander in darkness.

Strength discovery is the wakeup call leading to a godly legacy. Once the body of Christ understands their individualized blend of strengths, they are ready to make a collective decision to develop those talents and use them to glorify God. The joy of giving ignites a spark in our hearts and the hearts of others. God always gives His best and He expects the same from us.

The Law of Expedition: When we begin to search, we open the door of new possibilities and *wisdom's desire to reveal herself.*

*God always gives His best and
He expects the same from us.*

Chapter Six
Five Loaves and Two Fish

One of my son Dan's favorite children's books was "The Boy Who Gave His Lunch Away."[9] Dan enjoyed hearing the story over and over again. He identified with the young lad who went to hear Jesus teach. In this wonderful children's book, a child's mother packed lunch for her son and sent him on his way. Later on that day, the young boy found himself as God's chosen instrument to help Jesus provide a picnic for over 5,000 people, through the simple act of giving Jesus his lunch. This innocent child did not know how the Lord would feed the multitude; he simply wanted to help! I can only imagine the joy Jesus experienced from his humble offering.

The lesson of the mega picnic rings true throughout the ages: give what you have and God will amplify its impact.

The boy who gave his lunch away teaches us a powerful lesson. Our willingness to join Jesus in helping others is part of God's divine design for demonstrating His goodness. In the miracle of the loaves and fishes, God met the needs of all the people assembled, but there's more to the story. There were leftovers! According to the account in John, chapter 6, Jesus instructed the disciples to gather the left over pieces so that nothing would be wasted. Did you ever wonder what happened to the extra bread and fish? God provided more food than the crowd of over 5,000 people could eat. Since He does not waste anything, He had the disciples collect the residual and blessed more people. Perhaps they gave it to the poor, or they offered "doggie bags," or even provided a snack time at the end of the service. The lesson here is that blessings from God have an extended shelf life.

The lesson of the mega picnic rings true throughout the ages: *give what you have and God will amplify its impact.*

Building Spiritual Muscle

It is not enough to identify our strengths. "Personal stewardship" calls for both discovering and using God's best in our lives. The Lord entrusts us with talents and requires us to develop those talents and strengths through consistent use; He wants us to become stronger and more effective by building spiritual muscle. If I worked out only when I felt like it, I would be at the gym a few times a year! Through experience, I now recognize the most difficult element of physical fitness is getting started. Inertia is a strong force holding me back, just like gravity exerts a powerful restraint on the space shuttle. However, once you lift off the launch pad, the journey becomes much easier. When you first step out in faith to use a newly discovered talent, you may experience strong resistance. As you move past the initial force of gravity, the ascent becomes easier, and before you know it, you will effortlessly operate in your gifts as the effects of gravity give way to free flight.

Discipline is a vital part of building spiritual muscle. The more you exercise, the stronger you become. However, exercising is not enough.

Nutrition is also a vital part of building muscle. As you cooperate with God in the renewing of your mind, you promote spiritual health. Being careful about what you dwell on is essential for a healthy spiritual diet.

Faithful Stewardship

Stewardship is the act of being responsible and accountable for something that is given to us. As faithful stewards, it is our responsibility to take stock of our talents, assessing where, when, and how to use them, and then acting in such a way as to give our best to those who need a touch from God. We are God's workmanship, created in Christ Jesus to do good works that he prepared in advance for us to do (Ephesians, 2:10). Exercising our gifts strengthens and refines them, leading to effective service. Think about times when you

Our joy comes from what we give.

were extremely blessed by someone giving their best to you. This experience probably led to a grateful heart and thanksgiving for their valuable contribution.

As stewards, we look forward to hearing "well done, good and faithful servant" from the one who loves us most. Our joy comes from what we give. In 1 Thessalonians 2:19, the apostle Paul said: "For what is our hope, our joy, or the crown in which we will glory in the presence of our Lord Jesus when He comes? Is it not you?"

It is our joy to be a part of the Father's "Express Delivery System," bringing His good and perfect gifts to the door of those we serve.

It is our joy to be a part of the Father's "Express Delivery System," *bringing His good and perfect gifts* to the door of those we serve.

Chapter Seven
The Ultimate Makeover

Television makeover shows cover everything from homes to dogs. Some shows feature people makeovers. On these shows, it's amazing how a change of clothes and new hairstyle can make such an incredible difference.

Strength makeovers are even more impressive. Dramatic changes are realized when individuals who impose limitations on themselves begin to acknowledge and develop their God-given gifts. Individual stewardship calls for a candid recognition of talent mismanagement and a willingness to "try on" new strengths. Discarding old, worn out misperceptions about yourself is similar to parting with old shirts; they become too ugly to keep.

Trying on a new wardrobe manufactured from strengths may seem uncomfortable at first, but the custom fit and new look are stunning. It reminds me of an old church chorus, "The best thing in my life I ever did do was to take off the old robe and put on the new."

What is God's divine clothing design? It begins with custom measurements from the "Master Tailor." Your strength wardrobe is designed for the perfect, custom fit. It is manufactured from materials designed not to fade and is even fireproof. Once you try on God's new line of strength clothing, you will be impressed with both the comfort and durability. The Master Tailor's ingenious sense of fashion is never out of style. It's time to discard your worn out, unappealing character wardrobe and put on the new, custom-tailored look.

The Master Tailor's ingenious sense of fashion is never out of style.

"He gave me a crown of beauty instead of ashes, the oil of joy instead of mourning, and *a garment of praise* instead of a spirit of despair." Isaiah 61:3

PART THREE
Supercharged Community Stewardship

Chapter Eight
Community Discovery

"Supercharged community stewardship" helps us see God's reflection within the faith community. It has two essential elements. The first is helping others discover their God-given gifts through a strength-based assessment. The second is helping community members use those gifts to bring a touch of heaven to earth. The Lord called us to complement each other and work together in unity. The book of Acts provides us with evidence for how He supercharges unity within a faith community. This dynamic community of believers prayed together, ate together, took care of each other's needs, and found a compelling mission in bringing the message of salvation to the world.

A Community Parable

Once upon a time the animals decided they must do something heroic to meet the problems of a "new world," so they organized a school. They had adopted an activity curriculum consisting of running, climbing, swimming and flying. To make it easier to administer the curriculum, all the animals took all the subjects. The duck was excellent in swimming. In fact, he was better than his instructor. But he made only passing grades in flying and was very poor in running. Since he was slow in running, he had to stay after school and also drop swimming in order to practice running. This was kept up until his webbed feet were badly worn and he was only average in swimming. But average was acceptable in school so nobody worried about that, except the duck. The rabbit started at the top of the class in running but had a nervous breakdown because so much makeup work was required of him in swimming. The squirrel was excellent in climbing until he experienced frustration in the flying class where his teacher made him start from the ground up instead of the treetop down. He also developed a "charlie horse" from overexertion and then got a

"C" in climbing and "D" in running. The eagle was a problem student and was disciplined severely. In the climbing class, he beat all the others to the top of the tree but insisted on using his own way to get there.[10]

This parable by George Reavis speaks volumes about individual and community assessment. There are times when well-meaning people in our lives expect us to excel in areas of minimal strength. The lesson of the parable is to be who God made us to be; He designed us to flourish through the realization of our strengths. However, many of us have become discouraged trying to be something we are not.

There is another lesson from the parable. Specifically, it is what can be learned from how well the animals complemented each other. If the animals joined forces they would have a rich talent base for accomplishing much more than they could individually; they could realize the potential of community. This parable shares the essence of 1 Corinthians 12, where the Body of Christ is comprised of unique parts working interdependently with a common purpose. It represents unity through diversity and amplifies the importance of each individual part. We need each other. The community of believers is intentionally designed to flourish through meaningful, productive interdependent relationships. Strength renovation requires collaboration. The rebuilding of faith communities is the restoration of dynamic, respectful relationships among believers. Independence must give way to interdependence.

"Community discovery" is the art of helping others find and use their individual gifts and talents within their faith community. When it comes to bringing a touch of heaven to earth, the explosive energy of genuine faith community is truly more than the sum of the individual parts. Communities come alive through our connections to those we complement, and to those who complement us. This is the heart of God's design for presenting a brilliant light to the world. Once believers see each other within the Master Architect's plan, respect, appreciation, and love emerge. By this they will know we are his disciples, if we love one another (John 13:35).

The Power of Encouragement

"In the day I called, you answered me. You encouraged me with strength in my soul" (Psalms 138:3). As illustrated in this verse, encouragement builds us up; it inspires, renews, strengthens, and brings new hope. Encouragement infuses us with the strength needed to take risks and attempt something new. Community stewardship is all about helping others discover and use their gifts. Those who are limited by self-restrictive thinking need assistance to break out of their self-imposed prisons. They need someone to help them consider the possibility of being more than they presently are. They need the gift of encouragement.

Encouragement is grounded in a genuine, realistic appraisal of someone's ability. Parents understand the power of encouragement when they are coaching their little ones in the art of walking. Coaching begins when a child's parent recognizes she is ready to take her first step. They watch her crawl, lift herself up to the sofa, slowly easing herself down, and repeating these behaviors with increased excellence. One day, the parent takes their little one by both hands and gently leads her in the first steps. Every step forward is rewarded with exuberant praise.

    The power of encouragement is clearly revealed in how parents respond when the child falls. First, the child knows her parents love her and her attempts at walking; she is accustomed to their sounds of approval throughout the entire process. When she falls, the wise parent simply helps her up and offers as much support as she needs. The process continues until the child learns balance and masters walking. The Lord directs us to build each other up. Encouragement provides the gift of preventive medicine in that it keeps our hearts open and pliable.

"Each of us should please his neighbor for his good, to *build him up.*" Romans 15:2

"Encourage one another daily, as long as it is called "Today," so that none of you may be hardened by sin's deceitfulness."
Hebrews 3:13

The Power of Language

Our speech has great power to encourage or discourage. One may be quite skilled at not using negative words and less skilled in the use of encouraging words. Avoiding negative words is necessary, but not sufficient. Proverbs 27: 5 reminds us that open rebuke is better than hidden love. Our love for others must be verbalized and realized through action. The good news is that becoming skillful in the art of encouragement can be learned through the intentional use of uplifting words. Proverbs 12:18 gives excellent insight about the restorative benefits of well-chosen words: "Reckless words pierce like a sword, but the tongue of the wise brings healing." Moreover, our actions must resonate with our words. To counteract the "talk is cheap" dilemma, 1 John 3:18 directs us to love with our actions.

Teaching and Mentoring

Helping others discover and use their gifts is essential for group growth. "Discovery coaching" requires both encouragement and teaching. Within a community of believers, individuals who have a sound grasp of talent assessment and alignment are needed to help its members become good stewards of their God-given gifts. Training a group of people to use SHAPE, Network, Strengths Finder and the Values in Action survey will prove to be a wise investment toward assessing personal strengths. Community stewardship calls for wisdom to act as a guide in assisting each member to grow in their individual gifting. The Scriptural principle of interdependence found in 1 Corinthians 12 becomes transformational when each member knows who they are and how they fit into the community. Individual talents must not be hidden under a bushel — we need to know each other's strengths and have a formidable grasp of how to work in concert to fulfill God's plans.

Helping others discover and use their gifts is essential for group growth.

The Scriptural principle of interpersonal interdependence found in 1 Corinthians 12 becomes transformational when each member knows who they are and how they fit into the community.

The book of Acts provides us with evidence for how He supercharges unity within a faith community.

Chapter Nine
Community Coordination

Successful renovation calls for a coordinated effort. Project completion is carefully planned in phases for maximizing capital. Someone who understands the plan and how to coordinate resources oversees the project to ensure quality implementation. Renovating faith communities requires the same type of expertise. Community leadership acts as the project superintendent; they must have clear communication with the Master Architect and wisdom gained from participating in other building projects. They understand the following:

The Master Architect's Plan
Knowing the Master Architect and His plan for faith communities is essential to successful renovation. The plan has a clear goal of caring for both eternal

and temporal needs, and focuses on rebuilding lives. Open communication with the Master Architect ensures quality implementation.

Materials

Resources for the renovation are sometimes difficult to uncover, even though they reside within the community. The challenge is helping members discover the riches of their God-given gifts.

People

Understanding people and how to help them experience the joy of making a meaningful contribution is a key ingredient to successful renovation. Knowing how to balance challenge and support provides the right blend for realizing the best within the community.

Conflict Management

Whenever people come together, conflict emerges. Conflict has both positive and negative effects. Successfully managing conflict strengthens relationships, increases the quality of problem solving, and sets an example for productively working through differences.

The Unexpected

Expecting the unexpected gives one a strong advantage for project completion. Moving forward, there will be obstacles to overcome — it goes with the territory. An age-old axiom stands true: the more significant our progress, the stronger the resistance.

Quality Control

The ability to see and understand a faith community as a living system is a gift associated with effective administration. A renovation overseer views the entire project from all angles, without micromanaging. In fact, it is the antithesis of micromanagement. Instead, the renovator seeks to delegate the details and oversees the big picture.

Open communication with the Master
Architect ensures quality implementation.

Chapter Ten
Preventive Maintenance

"Preventive maintenance" requires strengthening a community in six areas. Strength in the following areas makes us resistant to deteriorating influences.

GRATITUDE:
- Noticing and being thankful for the numerous blessings in our lives
- Seeking ways to honor God through meaningful service

LOVE:
- Focusing on the needs of others
- Giving and receiving unconditional love

JOY:
- ❊ Experiencing joy
- ❊ Meaningful relationships with our brothers and sisters

PATIENCE:
- ❊ A willingness to wait for God's best
- ❊ Giving others the benefit of the doubt

PEACE:
- ❊ Experiencing a peace that passes understanding

FAITH:
- ❊ Trusting God with our lives
- ❊ Looking to God for help in our time of need

Preventive maintenance operates on the "nurturing principle." All of nature requires proper care for optimal growth. For example, if a plant does not receive adequate water, sunshine, and nutrients, it will die. The same principle applies to our relationships; they will deteriorate without proper care. Relationships thrive on exquisite care. When a couple takes each other for granted and neglect nurturing their relationship, love fades and their bond is compromised. However, if they are intentional about investing in the relationship, they will flourish. God's definition of love contains all the nutrients relationships need to flourish. He described love as patient, kind, not envious, boastful or proud. Love is not rude, it is not self-seeking, it is not easily angered, and it keeps no record of wrongs (1 Corinthians 13).

God's definition of love contains all
the nutrients we need to *flourish*.

Chapter Eleven
Optimal Growth

Since faith communities are living entities, they have the capacity for exquisite growth and development. God designed the Garden of Eden as a haven of superb health and beauty. Sin entered the garden, and the rest is history. But God restores us through Christ; we are a new creation in Him (2 Corinthians 5:17). When believers come together as new creations, they have the capacity to form a strong, influential community. The effects of sin will continue to wreak havoc with the magnificent potential in their midst; the key is found in their resolve to minimize sin's influence.

Traditional methods for dealing with sin involve preaching against it and focusing on how to avoid it. Another approach to minimizing sin's impact proves to be most helpful. When God's work is our top priority, there is little time or energy for sin. It reminds me of a story I heard once about a father who taught his daughter how to ride a bicycle. Father and daughter went to a large parking lot where she would have plenty of room. They went when the lot was virtually free of cars. His daughter kept saying she feared hitting one of the light poles in the lot. Her father told her not to focus on the pole; however, the girl kept talking about the light pole and sure enough, rode her bicycle right into the pole! Dwelling on sin takes us right into the light pole. Dwelling on God's plan leads us to our desired destination.

Natural Growth

The secret for optimal growth is found in our food source. Jesus revealed the ultimate spiritual food in the book of John, chapter 15. He spoke about the vine and the branches, giving us an illustration of how a branch and its fruit are supported by the vine. Jesus is the vine, we are the branches, and the fruit is what our lives produce. Nothing of significance can be done apart from Christ. Optimal growth depends on our relationship with the Vine. As believers, we open our lives to the Vine and His life flows through us. The vine and branches passage contains another valuable lesson.

The Power of Pruning

When the branches of a vine begin to grow, they spread out quickly; left unattended, vine branches increase and the quality of the fruit decreases. Similarly in our spiritual lives, it is easy to become overly involved with different activities, spreading ourselves too thin. Optimal growth requires pruning.[11] The quality of our growth is enhanced by cutting back on that which is not necessary, and by concentrating our efforts on a few activities that produce the best fruit. Discerning what is best comes from wisdom (Philippians 1:10); quality is more important than quantity. Understanding our talents and the talents of those within our faith community helps us focus on the best fruit possible. As believers open themselves to the Vine, they optimize growth and the quality of fruit.

Positivity

Positive psychology enhances our understanding of optimal growth. It is the study of what makes individuals and communities thrive. Research areas include gratitude, altruism, hope, optimism, wisdom, courage, and forgiveness.[12] In her landmark research, Barbara Fredrickson discovered a "Broaden and Build" effect related to positivity.[13] Positive emotions increase our peripheral vision and expand our thinking. Opening our hearts and minds leads to positive emotions that promote discovering and building new skills and knowledge. Positivity helps us find solutions for problems within our faith communities.

The famous "Nun Study" demonstrated how positivity is related to longevity. A group of nuns entering the convent wrote about their perceptions of their vocation. Those young women who used positive, hopeful words in their initial writings lived approximately ten years longer than those who did not demonstrate a sense of optimism.[14] Positivity also improves the quality of our emotional and physical health.[15] There is much to glean from the lessons of positive psychology for optimizing both individual and community growth.

Acting On What You Know

- ❂ Determine to focus more on strengths and less on weaknesses. See yourself and others from a strength-based perspective. Remember, you are a new creation in Christ.

- ❂ Use the suggested resources to discover your gifts.

- ❂ Use your gifts; as you exercise your talents, they will increase.

- ❂ Help others discover and use their gifts.

- ❂ Pray and trust God for supercharged results!

Renovation Reflections

If you've ever enjoyed the experience of seeing a major architectural renovation from beginning to end, or even a modest home remodel, the results can be breathtaking. Each time I visit the Vinoy in St. Petersburg, Florida, I always take time to look at the restoration photos they display in this unforgettable hotel. The care, finances, and amount of time invested in the restoration reminds me of the cost for restoring something to its original glory.

The Lord gave His life to restore us to Himself and to each other. His restoration brings us back to the original grandeur of man before the fall. Strength renovation is a type of restoration for the community of believers called the church; its goal is to restore the church to its original glory.

Strength renovation is both necessary and possible.

Conflict and division have tainted today's church. The light of many congregations has become dim through a deterioration of fellowship related to a deficit, faultfinding perspective; however, change is possible.

Repentance refers to a decision to change our thinking. The wonderful thing about repentance is that it is possible. You can choose to forgive and use your gifts in meaningful service. You can also choose to focus on the strengths in others and encourage them to use their gifts. Strength renovation is both necessary and possible.

My hope is for God's people to make a shift from a deficit-based perspective to one that is strength-based. Since you and I are a new creation in Christ, His image is reflected in all the good gifts, talents, and personality traits He pours into our lives. Even though we were once separated from God, He reconciled us to Himself through Christ. He commands us to be reconciled to each other and reflect His image through our strengths. It is time to increase the power of His light and shine as stars in the universe through strength renovation.

RESOURCES

1. "A. Marc Gillinov, MD." clevelandclinic.org. Cleveland Clinic, n.d. Web 7 July, 2010.

2. "Renaissance Vinoy Resort and Golf Club St. Petersburg, Florida." National Trust for Historic Preservation, n.d. Web. 12 July, 2010.

3. McGee, Robert. The Search for Significance. Nashville: Thomas Nelson, 2003. Print.

4. Synder, C. Richard. Handbook of Hope. Maryland Heights: MO: Academic Press, 2000. Print.

5. Bugbee, Bruce. Discover Your Spiritual Gifts the Network Way. Grand Rapids: Zondervan, 2005. Print.

6. Saddleback Church. Class 301: Shape. Lake Forest, CA: Saddleback Church. Print.

7. Raith, Tom. Strengthsfinder 2.0. Washington, DC: Gallup Press, 2007. Print.

8. Seligman, Martin and Peterson, Richard. Values in Action. viacharacter.org, n.d. Web. 17 August, 2010.

9. Hill, Dave and Wind, Betty. The Boy Who Gave His Lunch Away. St. Louis: Concordia Publishing House, 1970 Print.

10. Reavis, George. The Animal School. Peterborough: NH: Crystal Springs Books, 1999. Print.

11. Wilkinson, Bruce. Secrets of the Vine. New York:Multnomah, 2001. Print.

12. Snyder, C. Richard and Lopez, Shane. Positive Psychology: The Scientific and Practical Explorations of Human Strengths. Thousand Oaks, CA: Sage, 2007. Print.

13. Fredrickson, Barbara. Positivity. New York: Crown, 2009. Print.

14. Butler, S and Snowdon, D. "Trends in Mortality in Older Women: Findings from the Nun Study." Journal of Gerontology: Social Sciences 51B(4) (1996):201208, Print.

15. "Heart Disease." ScienceDaily 18 February 2010. Web. 17 August, 2010.

www.ingramcontent.com/pod-product-compliance
Lightning Source LLC
Chambersburg PA
CBHW030004050426
42451CB00006B/108